FOLLOW THAT FOOD

Buffy Silverman

Raintree
Chicago, Illinois

Designed by Michelle Lisseter and
Bridge Creative Services.
Picture Research by Hannah Taylor and Fiona Orbell.
Printed and bound in China by WKT Company
Limited.

11 10 09 08 07
10 9 8 7 6 5 4 3 2 1

**Library of Congress
Cataloging-in-Publication Data**
Silverman, Buffy.
  Follow that food / Buffy Silverman.
    p. cm.
  Includes bibliographical references and index.
  ISBN 1-4109-2595-1 (library binding-hardcover) --
ISBN 1-4109-2624-9 (pbk.)
  1. Pizza--Juvenile literature. I. Title.
  TX770.P58S556 2006
  641.8'248--dc22

                                    2006008785

13 digit ISBNs
978-1-4109-2595-4 (hardcover)
978-1-4109-2624-1 (paperback)

Acknowledgments
The author and publisher are grateful to the
following for permission to reproduce copyright
material: Alamy Images/Digital Archive Japan
p. **27**; Alamy Images/DIOMEDIA pp. **10–11**;
Anthony Blake Photo Library pp. **20–21** (David
Marsden), **24** (John Sims), **15** (Maximilian Stock
Ltd); Corbis pp. **12–13** (Ed Young); Corbis/Royalty
Free pp. **4–5**, **8**; Corbis/zefa pp. **22–23** (Daniel
Boschung); Getty Images/Photodisc p. **7**; Getty
Images/Stone p. **17**; Getty Images/The Image Bank
pp. **18–19**; Masterfile/JW pp. **16–17**.

Cover photographs of food reproduced with
permission of Getty Images/Photodisc.

Illustrations by Bridge Creative Services.

The publishers would like to thank Nancy Harris and
Daniel Block for their assistance in the preparation of
this book.

Every effort has been made to contact copyright
holders of any material reproduced in this book.
Any omissions will be rectified in subsequent
printings if notice is given to the publishers.

Contents

Some words are printed in bold, **like this**. You can find out what they mean on page 30. You can also look in the box at the bottom of the page where they first appear.

Follow That Food

The smell of baking pizza fills the air. You enter a **pizzeria** (pizza shop). You order your favorite pepperoni pizza. Pepperoni is a spicy sausage. You sniff. Your stomach rumbles. Finally, the server brings the pizza.

You pick up a slice and take a bite. It's delicious! As you eat, you think about your pizza. You can see the kitchen where the pizza was made. Inside is the oven that baked it.

Have you ever wondered where your pizza came from? Where did the restaurant get what it needed to make your pizza? Did everything come directly from one farm? How did that pizza get to you?

pizzeria   place where pizzas are made and sold

▼ We all like to eat pizza. But where does the pizza come from?

Take a bite!

You take one bite after another. You eat crust, sauce, cheese, and pepperoni.

Each **ingredient** needed to make the pizza came from a different place. Different **factories** made the ingredients. One factory made tomato sauce. It used tomatoes grown on a farm. Another factory made cheese. It used milk from a **dairy farm**. A dairy farm is a farm that raises cows for their milk.

Some of the ingredients came from nearby farms. Others came from far away.

> ## Pizza history
>
> *In 1889, a chef created a special pizza. He made it for the queen of Italy. He topped the pizza with the colors of the Italian flag. He used red tomatoes and white cheese. He added a green **herb** plant called basil to make it tasty. He made the first cheese and tomato pizza.*

You take a bite of pizza. ▶ It's delicious! You taste cheese and pepperoni.

dairy farm	farm that raises cows for their milk
factory	place where goods are made
herb	plant used to flavor food
ingredient	item needed to make something

From Wheat to Crust

Every pizza begins with a crust. Flour is the main **ingredient** in crust. The flour in most pizzas is made from **wheat**. Wheat is a kind of grass.

Farmers grow wheat in fields. The wheat grows tall. **Grain** grows at the top of the wheat stalk. Grain is the small, hard part of the wheat where the seeds are. When the wheat is ripe, machines **harvest** (gather) the grain.

Ripe wheat is harvested ▼ in a field. Big machines cut the grain off the top of the wheat stalk.

grain	small, hard part of wheat and other grasses
harvest	to gather a crop
wheat	kind of grass grown around the world

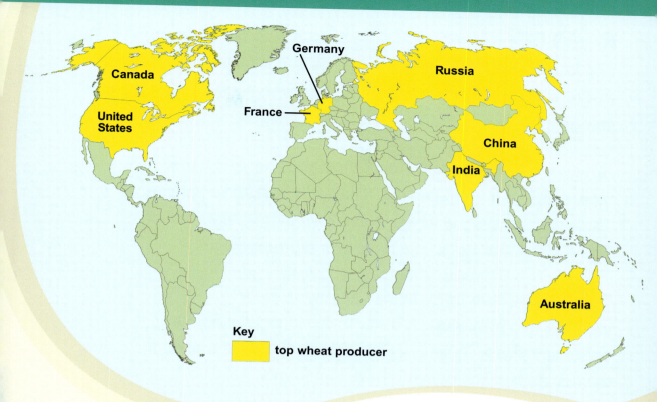

Key

top wheat producer

▲ All over the world, farmers grow wheat. Most of the world's wheat comes from a few countries. China, India, the United States, Russia, Australia, Canada, France, and Germany grow the most wheat.

First farmers

People have eaten wheat for thousands of years. They picked wild wheat. About 10,000 years ago, people started planting wheat. They grew wheat where they lived. They did not need to search for food as much.

At the mill

The **harvested wheat** is taken to a **mill**. It is taken in trucks, trains, and boats. A mill is a place where **grain** is ground into flour.

How is wheat turned into flour? First, the grain is cleaned. Stones and dust are taken out. Then, it is soaked in water. The water softens the wheat. Next, rollers crush the wheat. This turns it into flour. The flour is put into packages.

Trucks carry flour from the mill. It goes to stores, bakeries, and **pizzerias**. A baker makes dough with flour, water, and **yeast**. Yeast is a special ingredient that makes the dough rise. The dough is baked into crust.

It's alive!

*To make crust or bread, bakers need yeast. Yeast is alive. Just like us, yeast breathes air. When yeast breathes, it gives off **carbon dioxide** gas. The gas bubbles make dough rise.*

carbon dioxide	gas released into the air by plants and animals
mill	place where grain is ground into flour
yeast	living thing used to make bread and crust

◀ Wheat is poured from a truck. It is ground into flour at a mill.

On the Tomato Trail

What goes on top of pizza crust? Most people like tomato sauce. A cook can spread sauce on a pizza crust in a few seconds. But it takes a long time to make the sauce.

Farmers plant tomato seeds in their fields. Tomato vines grow from the seeds. The vines grow tall. Yellow flowers bloom. Tiny green tomatoes grow from the flowers. In the warm sun, tomatoes turn red.

When tomatoes are ripe, huge machines cut the vines. Machines shake the tomatoes off the vines and load them onto a truck.

Tomatoes grow best in warm places. In the United States, a lot of tomatoes grow in California.

Pricey pizza

*Why would rainy weather in California make your pizza cost more? If a lot of rain falls, fewer tomatoes can be picked. Many tomatoes **rot** or go bad on the vine. The price of sauce goes up with fewer tomatoes.*

rot to go bad

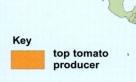

California — United States

Italy

Turkey

China

India

Egypt

▲ The United States, China, Turkey, Italy, Egypt, and India grow the most tomatoes.

13

Harvested tomatoes are ▶ loaded on trucks. The trucks bring the tomatoes to a **factory**. At the factory, they are made into sauce.

Stir that sauce

A **cannery** is a place where food is put in cans. At a cannery, tomatoes are washed. They are then peeled and chopped. Chopped tomatoes are cooked in huge pots. The sauce thickens as water boils out. **Herb** and **spice** plants are added. They flavor the food. The sauce is poured into cans. It is shipped to stores, restaurants, and **pizzerias**.

Today, farmers around the world grow tomatoes. Hundreds of years ago, the only tomatoes were wild ones. They grew in South America and Mexico (see map on p28).

Spain is a country in Europe. Spanish people came to Mexico around 1518. They had never seen tomatoes. They brought tomato seeds back with them to Spain.

Soon tomatoes were grown all over Europe. At first, people thought tomatoes were bad for you. They would not eat them. It took 100 years for tomatoes to become a popular food in Europe.

A cook checks the ▶ tomato sauce. After the sauce thickens, it is put in cans.

cannery	place where food is put in cans
spice	plant that adds flavor to food

Cheese, Please!

Bite into a slice of pizza. Warm cheese stretches from the pizza to your mouth. Where does that stringy cheese begin?

Milk is used to make cheese. Milk for cheese usually comes from a cow. Sometimes it may come from a goat or sheep.

Every day a cow eats ▶ about 90 pounds (40 kilograms) of grass, hay, and corn.

On a **dairy farm**, cows eat grass, hay, and corn. They also drink a lot of water. Cows need a lot of food and water to make milk.

A farmer brings the cows to the milking parlor. Each cow is hooked up to a milking machine. The machine pumps the milk into clean containers. Milk is kept in a cool place. A refrigerated truck carries the milk from the farm.

Thirsty cows

Every day, a cow drinks as much water as one bathtub would hold.

Cows are milked two or ▲ three times a day. One cow can produce 8 gallons (30 liters) of milk a day.

Curds and whey

How is cheese made out of milk? To turn milk into cheese, liquid must be taken out of it.

In a cheese **factory**, milk is heated. The cheese maker adds a chemical called **rennet**. Rennet comes from a cow's stomach. It makes the warm milk thicken. The milk forms chunks. The chunks are called **curds**. A watery liquid called **whey** also forms.

The cheese maker pours out the whey. Then, they cut up the curds. When more whey comes out, the cheese maker pours it off. Finally, the cheese is solid.

Cheese facts

A long time ago, tribes in the Middle East carried milk in bags. The bags were made from sheep's stomachs. The stomachs had rennet in them. The desert heat warmed the milk. The rennet turned the warm milk into curds. That chunky milk was the first cheese.

curd	part of milk that turns solid
rennet	chemical from a cow's stomach that makes milk form into curds and whey
whey	watery part of milk

▲ Cheese curds ripen at a cheese factory. It takes many weeks or months to make cheese.

Make it mozzarella

What is the perfect cheese for pizza? Soft, stretchy **mozzarella** cheese!

Who made the first mozzarella? People think mozzarella was made by accident. An Italian cheese maker was making **curds**. Curds are the part of milk that turn solid. He dropped some curds in hot water. When he took them out, they were soft and stretchy. The hot water had changed them. The cheese he made from the soft curds was the first mozzarella.

Today, mozzarella is still made when curds are stretched in hot water. The soft curds are then pressed into balls. The cheese rests for three or four weeks. Often, it is turned into shredded cheese. Then, it is packaged. Trucks bring it to stores and **pizzerias**.

Cheese lovers

In France, a person eats more than 45 pounds (20 kilograms) of cheese a year. French cheese makers make 400 kinds of cheese.

mozzarella   stringy cheese that is often melted on top of pizza

▼ You can buy many kinds of cheeses such as this mozzarella at a grocery store. What is your favorite cheese?

Toppings!

What is your favorite pizza topping? Do you like peppers and onions? Maybe you love extra cheese or mushrooms. In the United States, many people prefer **pepperoni**. Americans eat more than 250 million pounds (113 million kilograms) of pepperoni each year!

Do you like pepperoni? ▶
The pepperoni that we eat on pizza comes from hogs such as these.

butcher   person who prepares meat

Pepperoni is made from pork. On a hog farm, farmers raise hogs. The hogs sleep in sheds. They dig nests in straw where they sleep. Farmers feed them **wheat** and corn. They also feed them other **grains** such as barley and oats. To keep hogs healthy, farmers keep the sheds clean.

When hogs are grown, they are loaded onto trucks. Trucks carry them to a plant. At the plant, the hogs are killed. Their bodies are kept in a refrigerated room. **Butchers** cut meat off the hogs. Some of the meat is sent to sausage makers.

Hogs, hogs, hogs

Fifteen million hogs live on farms in Iowa. That is five times as many hogs as people in that state!

23

At a factory, pork ▶ sausages are hung to dry.

casing	bag made of animal intestine
curing	preserving meat by adding salt and drying it
germ	tiny living thing that spoils food and causes diseases
intestine	tube inside the body where food is broken down

Pass the pepperoni

A long time ago, people needed a way to store meat. There were no refrigerators. If meat is not kept cold, it **rots**. **Germs** grow in the meat. Germs are tiny living things that can spoil meat and cause diseases.

People learned to keep their meat longer. This is called **curing** it. First, they put salt on it. The salt killed germs. Then, they hung the meat to dry. Without water, germs could not live in the meat.

Today, sausages are often made in **factories**. At a factory, meat is ground up. Workers pour salt on the meat. Then, they add **herbs** and **spices**. Garlic and pepper give **pepperoni** sausage its special taste. Workers stuff the meat in **casings**. Casings are bags made of animal **intestines**. Intestines are a long tube inside the body. Food is broken down in the intestines. The sausages are hung to dry. Trucks carry sausages to stores.

Sausage story

Four thousand years ago, people in Iraq made the first sausages. They stuffed cured meat and herbs and spices into bags. The bags were made of animal intestines.

25

Pizza around the world

Have you ever eaten pizza with eggs cooked on top? You might if you lived in Australia! What you eat on your pizza depends on where you live. People around the world eat different foods. They put different foods on top of pizzas.

Japanese people live on islands. They are surrounded by water. Many people catch fish. In Japan, people eat a lot of seafood. They make pizza with shrimp, clams, and other seafood.

People in India cook spicy food. They put green **chilies** (hot peppers) on pizza. Instead of **mozzarella**, they use an Indian cheese called *paneer*. *Paneer* is a soft, white cheese similar to cottage cheese.

In France, people eat a pizza called *flambée*. It is topped with bacon, onion, and fresh cream.

Many different toppings ▶ are used on pizza, including seafood.

chili   hot pepper used for cooking

From the Farm to You

All of the **ingredients** for pizza travel from farms to factories. Railroad cars carry **wheat** to **mills**. Trucks filled with tomatoes drive long distances. Refrigerated trucks bring milk to a cheese **factory**. The cheese travels around the world on boats, trains, and airplanes. Truck drivers bring pepperoni to stores.

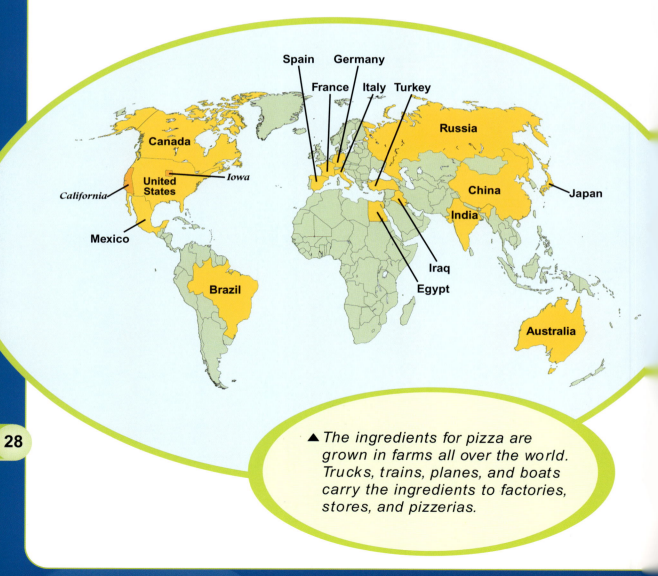

Spain   Germany
France   Italy   Turkey
Russia
Canada
Iowa
United States
California
China
Japan
India
Mexico
Iraq
Brazil
Egypt
Australia

▲ *The ingredients for pizza are grown in farms all over the world. Trucks, trains, planes, and boats carry the ingredients to factories, stores, and pizzerias.*

Many people help make the pizza you eat:

Farmers grow wheat.

Mill workers grind the wheat into flour that makes the crust.

Farmers grow tomatoes and **herbs**.

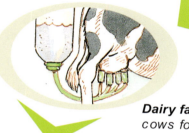

Factory workers cook the tomatoes and can them.

Dairy farmers raise cows for milk.

Cheese makers turn the milk into cheese.

Your pepperoni might have come from a hog farm in Iowa.

A cook puts sauce on the crust. She covers it with cheese and pepperoni.

When it is baked, the server brings it to you.

Glossary

butcher person who prepares meat. Butchers cut meat that is made into sausages.

cannery place where food is put in cans. Tomato sauce is put in cans at a cannery.

carbon dioxide gas released into the air by plants and animals. We breathe out carbon dioxide.

casing bag made of animal intestine. Sausage meat is stuffed in casings.

chili hot pepper used for cooking. Some people eat chilies on pizza.

curd part of milk that turns solid. Cheese is made from curds.

curing preserving meat by adding salt and drying it. Sausage meat is cured.

dairy farm farm that raises cows for their milk. Milk from a dairy farm can be made into cheese.

factory place where goods are made. Cheese is made at a cheese factory.

germ tiny living thing that spoils food and causes diseases. Germs in meat are killed before meat is made into sausage.

grain small, hard part of wheat and other grasses. When grains are ground, they make flour.

harvest to gather a crop. Big machines harvest wheat.

herb plant used to flavor food. Basil is a common herb.

ingredient item needed to make something. Wheat is an ingredient of pizza crust.

intestine tube inside the body where food is broken down. People sometimes use animal intestines when making sausage.

mill place where grain is ground into flour. Machines crush wheat at a mill.

mozzarella stringy cheese that is often melted on top of pizza. Mozzarella is made from milk.

pizzeria place where pizzas are made and sold. People eat pizzas at a pizzeria.

rennet chemical from a cow's stomach that makes milk form into curds and whey. Rennet is used to make cheese.

rot to go bad. When germs grow in food, it rots.

spice plant that adds flavor to food. A cook adds spices to tomato sauce.

wheat kind of grass grown around the world. Wheat is ground into flour.

whey watery part of milk. When people make cheese, they remove the whey.

yeast living thing used to make bread and crust. Yeast helps bread or crust rise.

Want to Know More?

Books to read

- Jones, Carol. *Cheese (From Farm to You)*. New York: Chelsea House Publications, 2002.
- Jones, Carol. *Pasta and Noodles (From Farm to You)*. New York: Chelsea House Publications, 2003.
- Watertown, Elaine Landau. *Popcorn!* Massachusetts: Charlesbridge Publishing, 2003.
- Honesdale, Cris Peterson. *Extra Cheese, Please!: Mozzarella's Journey from Cow to Pizza*. Pennsylvania: Boyds Mills Press, 2004.

Websites

- http://www.mda.state.mi.us/kids/pictures/dairy
  This website shows photographs of how cows are raised and milked.
- http://www.foodmuseum.com/pizzaingredients.html
  At this site, find more information about everything in a pizza.
- http://www.thepizzafarm.com/edu/kids_stuff.php
  At this site, visit a pizza farm that grows all the ingredients on a pizza.

Learn all about microbes that cause disease in **World's Worst Germs**.

Rotting is the last stage in a food chain that starts with plants. Find out more in **Shark Snacks**.

Index